**Barbara Guth Worlds of Wonder Science
Series for Young Readers**

UFOhs!

MYSTERIES IN THE SKY

Deborah Blumenthal & Ralph Blumenthal

ILLUSTRATIONS BY Adam Gustavson

UNIVERSITY OF NEW MEXICO PRESS | ALBUQUERQUE

One night in Florida when he was playing tennis,
something made Wes look up at the sky.

He held his breath.

A thing as big as a car
was *floating* in the air
above the lights of the tennis court.

It was oval-shaped,
with flashing lights,
red and blue.

Wes stared.

So did his friend Ken.
So did two grown-ups on the next court.

The thing flew closer to them
and then . . . suddenly . . .
shot out of sight and . . .
disappeared!

What was *that*?" Wes asked the grown-ups.

They shook their heads.

Wes and his friend ran back to Wes's house,
shouting,
"*We just saw a UFO!*"

Farmers,
fishermen,
pilots,
police,
and schoolchildren
from all over the world,
in small towns
and big cities,
have told the same story
again and again.

Out of the blue
or black night sky,
they looked up
and saw strange and wondrous things
they had never seen before.

What do we usually see
when we look in the sky?
Planes.
Birds,
the sun, clouds,
the moon and stars.
Even a comet.
All the things that belong in the sky.

But some people see fiery pin dots of flickering lights,
like blobs,
or fireballs,
or triangles,
or other things
with windows
zigzagging across the sky this way and that,
faster
than jets,
faster
faster
faster
than even shooting stars.

They'd dance madly through the air
like flickering fireflies,
sometimes swooping
close to the ground
or above the treetops
or ocean waves.

Or they'd land softly
on the ground
with a windy whirring sound
or no sound at all.

People who saw them
rushed to call
friends,
neighbors,
the police,
the Air Force.

DID YOU SEE WHAT I SAW?

What *are* these strange things?
They wanted to know.

Some people call them . . . Flying Saucers!

But real saucers don't fly around in the sky.
They stay home and hold teacups.

So there's a better name.
Unidentified Flying Objects.

UFOs!

What are they?
It's a mystery.
Where do they come from?
Another mystery.

Government people call them another name.
Unidentified Aerial Phenomena.
UAPs.
Phenomena is just an old Greek word
that means . . . *things that appear.*
Aerial means . . . *in the air.*
And unidentified means . . . *we don't know.*

But cattle, birds, dogs, and cats
raise their eyes and ears when
UFOs are near.
They even howl.
Cows moo and huddle together.

In Zimbabwe,
a country in southern Africa,
children were outside playing in the school yard
when they saw something round land near them.
None of the children knew about UFOs.

"Draw pictures of them," the grown-ups said.
So they did.
And the pictures looked the same.

Some people don't believe they are real.

But . . .

People who've seen them
have taken pictures of them.

And Navy pilots have made videos
and snapped photos out of their cockpits
when they're way up in the sky.

UFOs have even been seen
going into and out of the water!

But where do they come from?
It's a mystery.

And they're not all the same.

Some are round,

others look like pizza slices.

Or sausages.

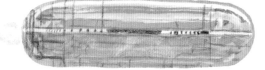

Or other different shapes.

They may have been around for a long, long time.

Years ago in Roswell, New Mexico,
something fell from the sky onto a ranch.
The rancher didn't have a camera,
but he stored the pieces until he was able
to get in touch with the local sheriff.

People from the Air Force
picked them up
then gave them to their commanders.

Was it really a UFO?
The Air Force said
yes.
Then, no,
it was
just . . .
. . . a crashed weather balloon.
Or maybe some kind of spying machine.

The only thing we know for sure
is that it didn't come from the ranch.

Again and again,
all over the world
people see things
in the sky
they can't explain.

In 2019,
in just the United States and Canada,
the number reached
six thousand!
Are they *all* UFOs?
Probably not.

Many might be reflections.
Planes,
satellites,
drones,
missile tests,
or the planet Venus,
the second from the sun,
which is brighter than every star
except the sun.

Can you think of other things they might be?

Could UFOs come from right here on earth,
as some people think?

Or from somewhere else?

But where?
What do you think when you look up in the sky?

Have YOU ever seen a UFO?
Would you like to?
What would you say if you did?

For now, they are mysteries in
the sky.

But some day?
Who knows?

Authors' Note

Why write a picture book about something we don't understand?
Why puzzle over Unidentified Flying Objects—a mystery to today's scientists, pilots, generals, journalists, teachers, librarians, and our earliest ancestors from the time of the caveman?

Because human beings are curious. We are born to wonder.

So when ancient people saw things in the sky that they couldn't understand, they made notes, or rather scratched images into rocks and wrote down stories. Today, we continue to explore our home planet and beyond—distant galaxies that take us back like time machines to the dawn of creation.

Astronauts orbit the earth to step foot on the moon again, and perhaps other worlds. But UFOs remain a mystery.

We do keep learning more. And now we know that our government has been studying them too. On the front page of the *New York Times* in December of 2017, Ralph and other reporters told how Navy pilots and their instruments captured images and electronic footprints of so-called Unidentified Aerial Phenomena—UAPs. And an official report in 2021 said most "probably do represent physical objects." So the government confirmed, they are real.

More than that? No one yet really knows.

So why did we write a book with more questions than answers? To get us thinking, not only about the mystery of UFOs, but also how much there is yet to discover about the entire cosmos.

(And yes, Wes and Ken are real people.)

FOR MORE INFORMATION ON UFOS

Harris, Shane. "UFO hearing features historic testimony from Pentagon officials." *Washington Post*, May 17, 2022, https://www.washington post.com/national-security/2022/05/17/ufo-hearing-congress/.

Kean, Leslie. *UFOs: Generals, Pilots, and Government Officials Go on the Record* (New York: Three Rivers Press, 2011).

Office of the Director of National Intelligence. "Preliminary Assessment: Unidentified Aerial Phenomena." June 25, 2021, https://www.dni.gov/files/ODNI/documents/assessments/Prelimary-Assessment-UAP-20210625.pdf.

Deborah Blumenthal is an award-winning journalist and the author of twenty-seven books for children and adults. She was a regular contributor to the *New York Times* and wrote beauty and fitness columns for the *Sunday Times* magazine. Her recent picture books include *Saving Stella: A Dog's Dramatic Escape from War*, the true story of a Syrian musician who rescued his dog from the fighting in Syria, and biographies of fashion icons Diana Vreeland and Iris Apfel, as well as architect Frank Gehry.

Ralph Blumenthal reported for the *New York Times* from 1964 to 2009 and has contributed recent articles on UFOs. He is the author of five nonfiction books, including *The Believer: Alien Encounters, Hard Science, and the Passion of John Mack*, which is about a Harvard psychiatrist who investigated UFO phenomena. Wes and Ken, the characters in the beginning of *UFOhs!*, are real people cited in *The Believer*.

ISBN 978-0-8263-6495-1 (cloth)
ISBN 978-0-8263-6496-8 (e-book)

Library of Congress Cataloging-in-Publication data is on file with the Library of Congress.

Founded in 1889, the University of New Mexico sits on the traditional homelands of the Pueblo of Sandia. The original peoples of New Mexico—Pueblo, Navajo, and Apache—since time immemorial have deep connections to the land and have made significant contributions to the broader community statewide. We honor the land itself and those who remain stewards of this land throughout the generations and also acknowledge our committed relationship to Indigenous peoples. We gratefully recognize our history.

Cover illustration by Adam Gustavson
Designed by Felicia Cedillos
Composed in Chapparal Pro 14/19